100 Hymns
With Just 3 Chords

Table Of Contents

Abide With Me

Alleluia! The Strife Is O'er

With praise

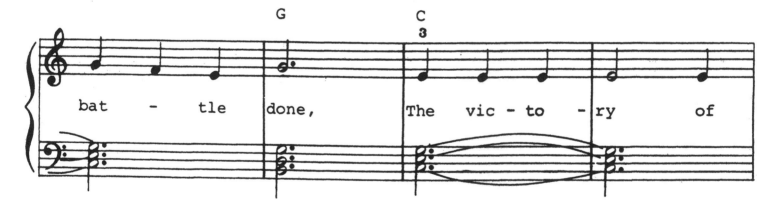

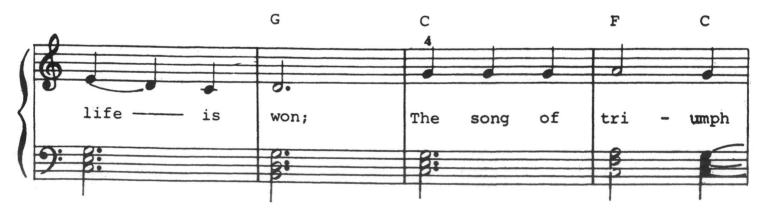

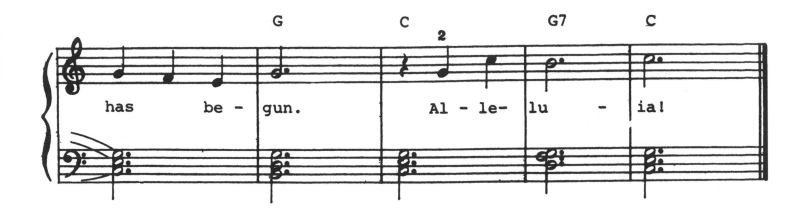

has be - gun.   Al - le - lu - ia!

I Love Thy Kingdom, Lord

With dignity

I love Thy king - dom, Lord, The

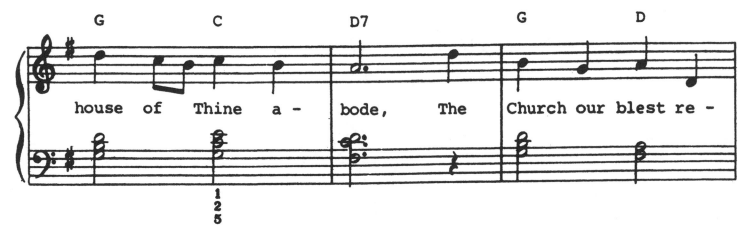

house of Thine a - bode, The Church our blest re -

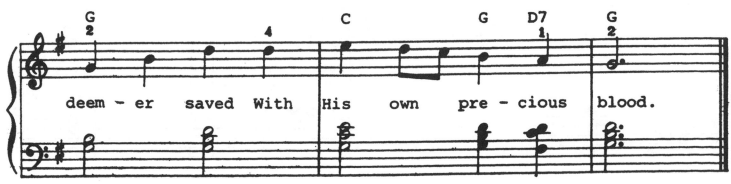

deem - er saved With His own pre - cious blood.

Adeste Fideles

(COME, ALL YE FAITHFUL)

O come, all ye faith - ful, Joy - ful and tri - umph - ant, O

come ye, O come ye to Beth - le - hem. Come and be - hold Him,

Born the King of an - gels, O come, let us a - dore Him, O come, let us a -

dore, Him O come, let us a - dore Him Christ the Lord.

All Hail The Power
Of Jesus' Name

Majestically

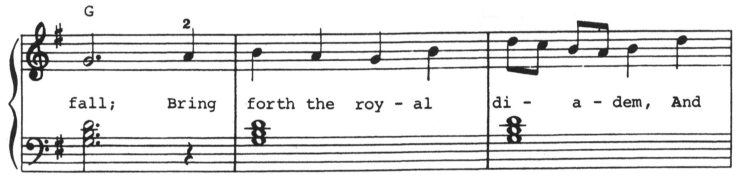

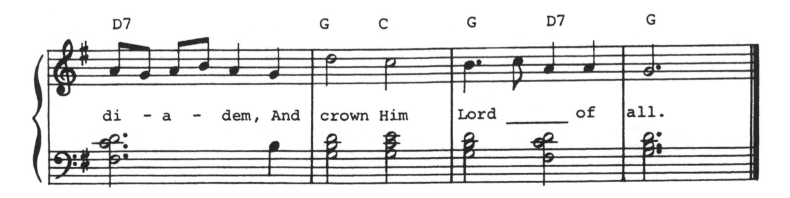

Amazing Grace

Moderato

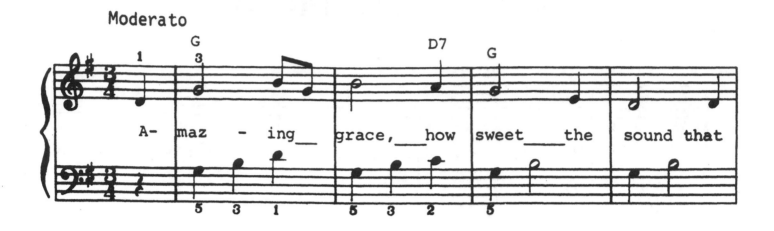

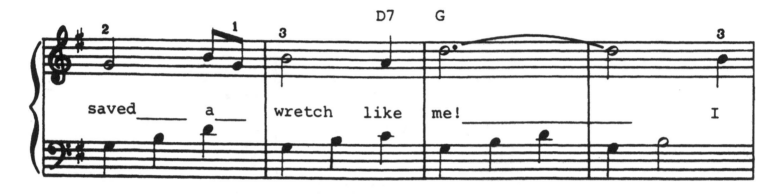

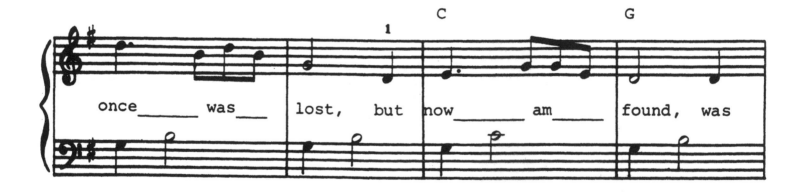

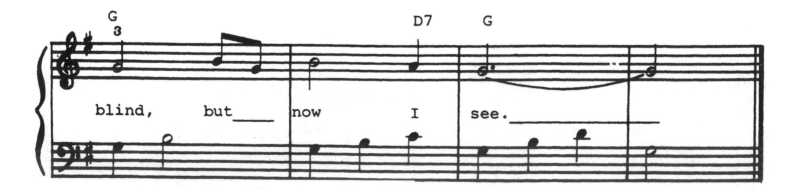

All Through The Night

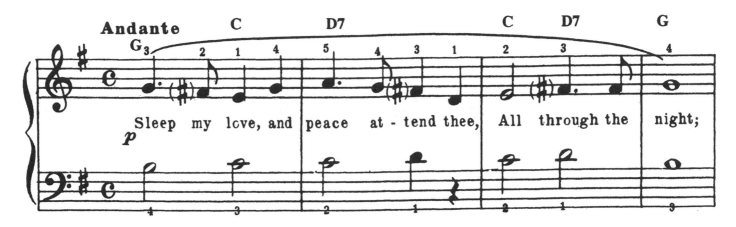

America

Moderato

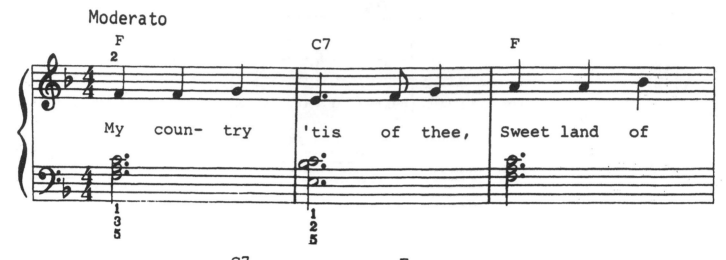

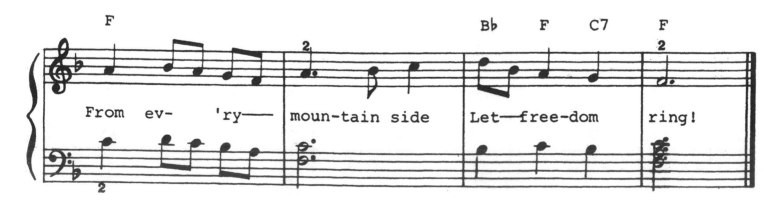

Art Thou Weary?

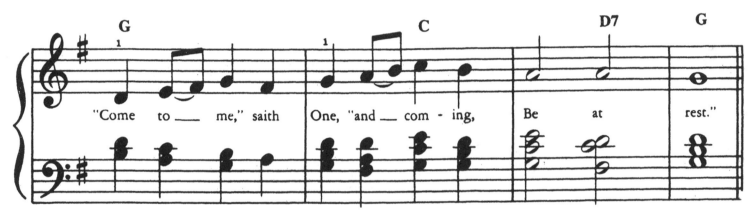

As Pants The Heart

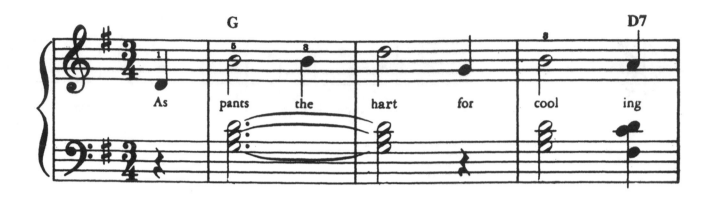

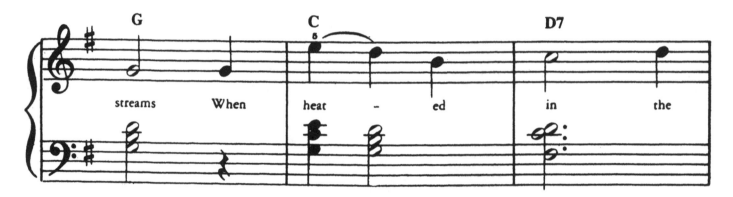

At The Cross

Away In A Manger

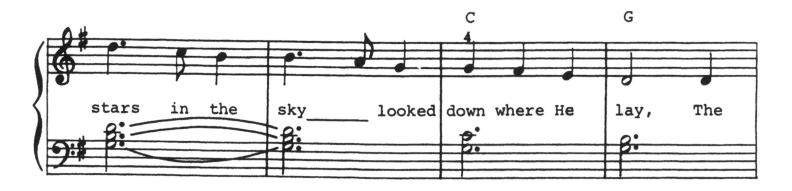

Be Thou Near, Dear Lord

Blessed Assurance

2nd time:

Blessed admission, perfect delight,
Visions of rapture now burst on my sight.
Angels descending bring from above,
Echoes of mercy, whispers of love.

(Repeat "This is my story" etc)

Blest Be The Tie

Moderato

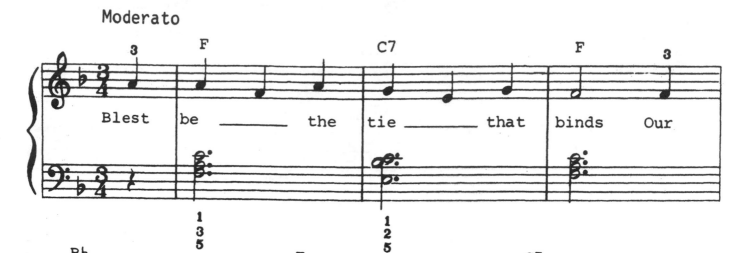

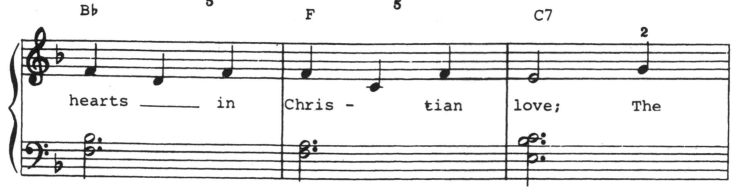

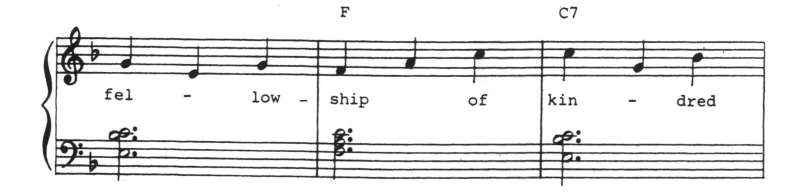

Christ The Lord Is Risen Today

Church In The Wildwood

There's a church in the val-ley by the wild-wood, No lov-li-er place in the

dale; No — spot is so dear to my child-hood As the

lit-tle brown church in the vale. O — come, come, come, come,

come to the church in the wild-wood, Oh, come to the church in the

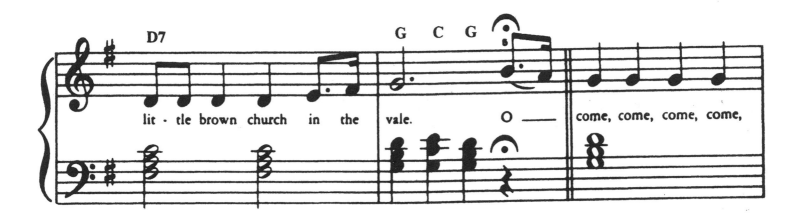

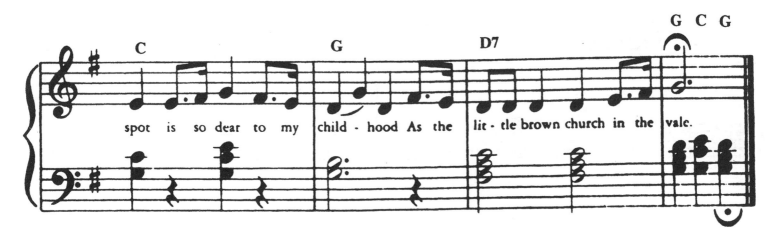

Come Thou Almighty King

Come, Thou Fount

Come, Ye Disconsolate

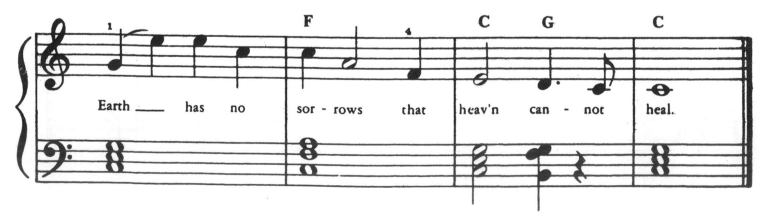

The Day Of Resurrection

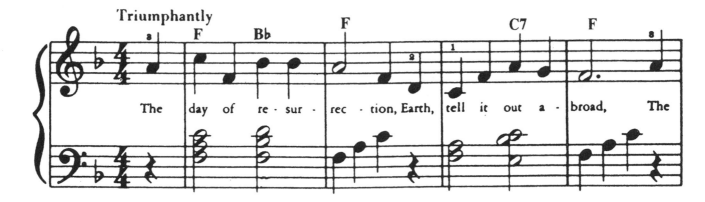

Fairest Lord Jesus

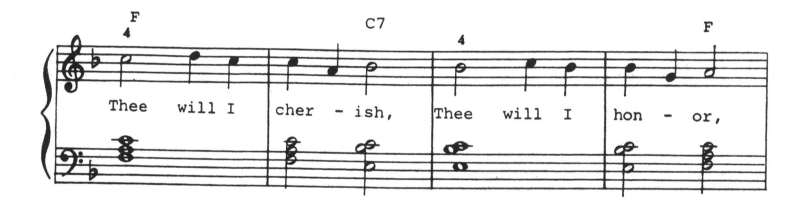

From Every Stormy Wind That Blows

Moderato

From ___ ev - 'ry storm - y wind that

blows, From ___ ev - 'ry swell - ing tide of

woes, There is a calm, a sure re- treat; 'Tis ___

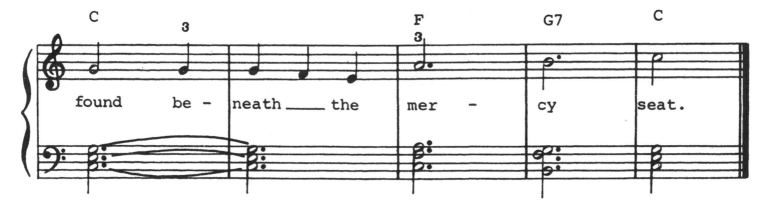

found be - neath ___ the mer - cy seat.

The First Noel

Once He Came In Blessing

God Be With You
Till We Meet Again

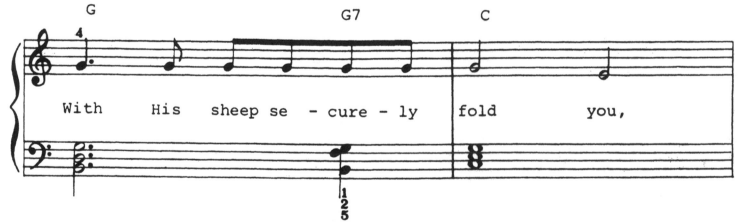

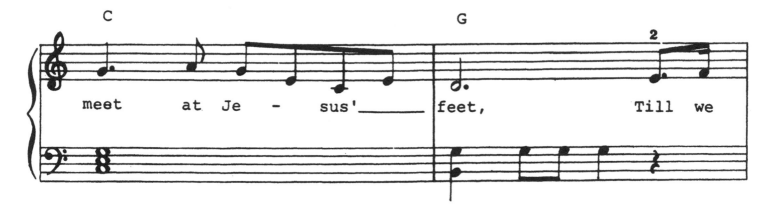

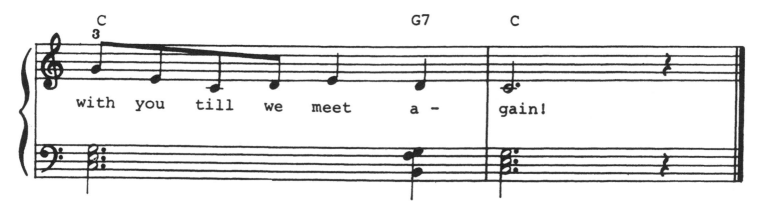

Go To Dark Gethsemane

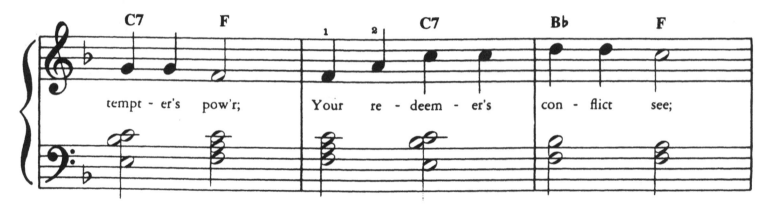

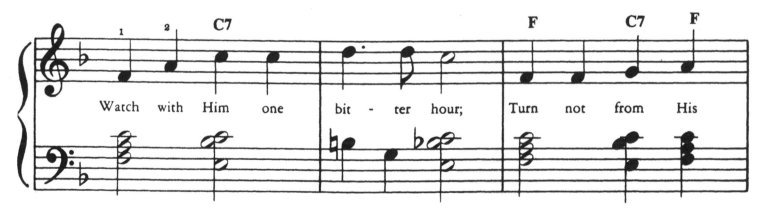

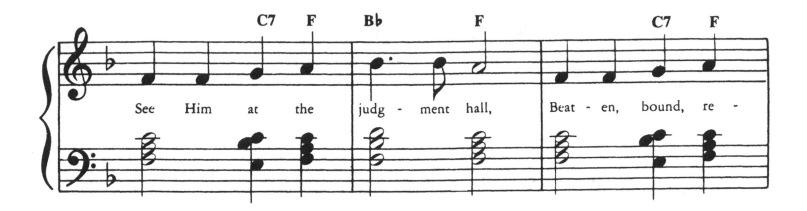

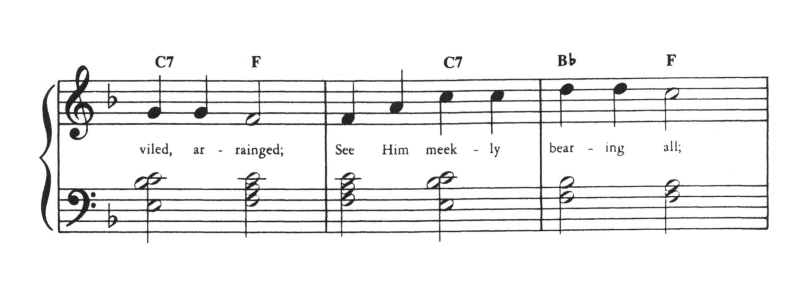

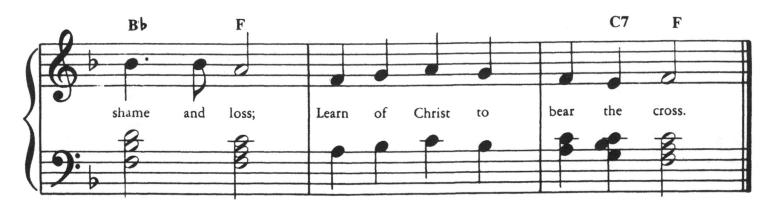

Glory To His Name

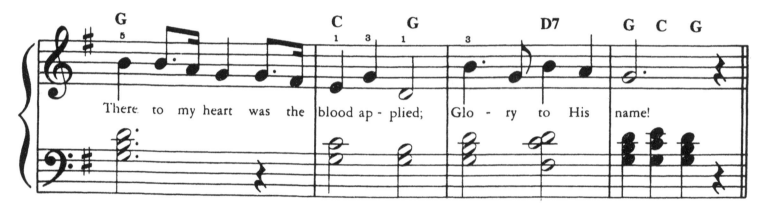

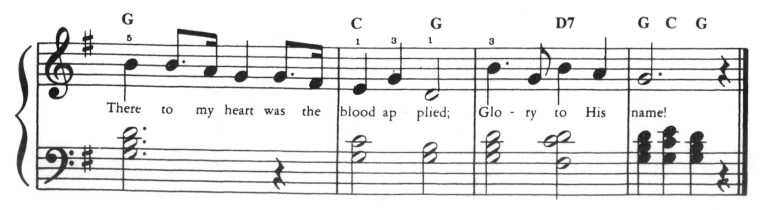

The Great Speckled Bird

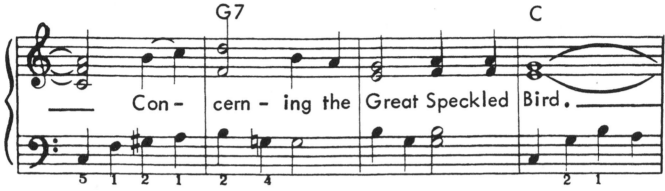

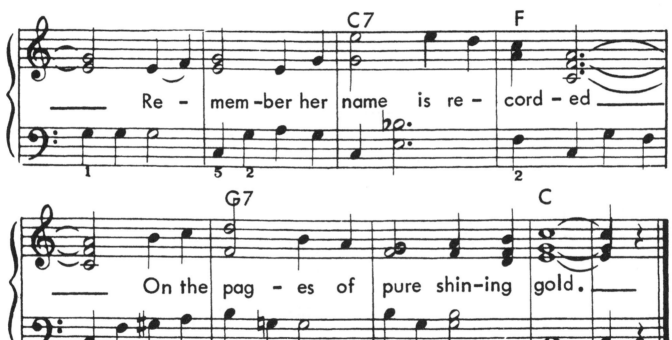

2. All the other birds flock all around her,
   But she is despised by the squad.
   Oh the Great Speckled Bird in the bible
   Is the one with the great church of God.

3. When He cometh descending from Heaven,
   On the cloud, as He wrote in His word,
   I'll be joyfully carried up to meet Him —
   On the wings of the Great Speckled Bird.

Guide Me, O Thou Great Jehovah

The Happy Life

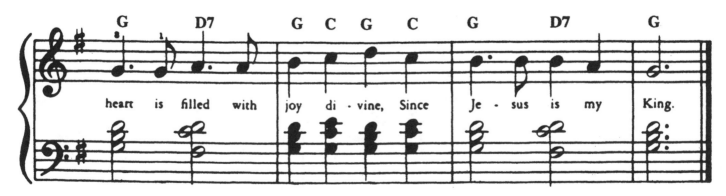

Hallelujah, He Is Risen

(Easter)

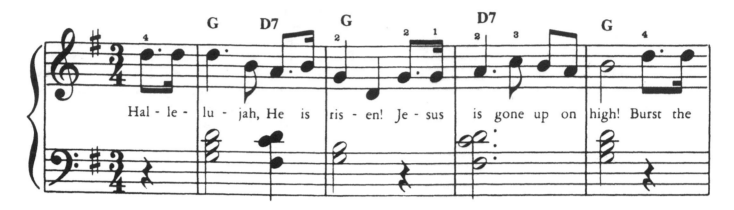

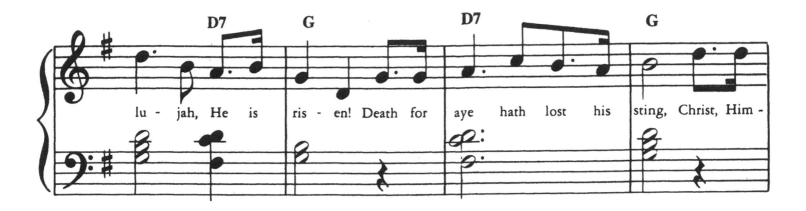

Hark, The Herald Angels Sing

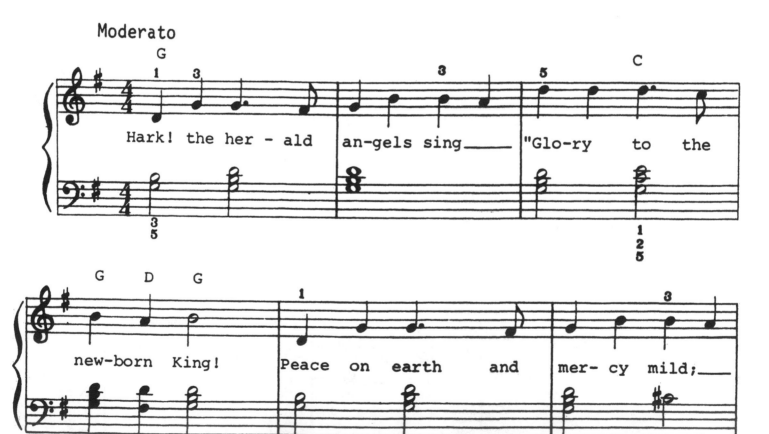

Moderato

Hark! the her - ald an-gels sing___ "Glo-ry to the new-born King! Peace on earth and mer- cy mild;___

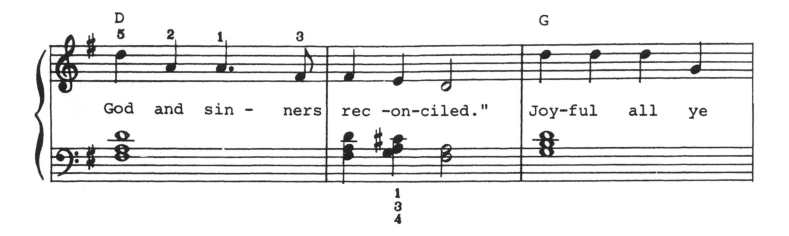

God and sin - ners rec -on-ciled." Joy-ful all ye

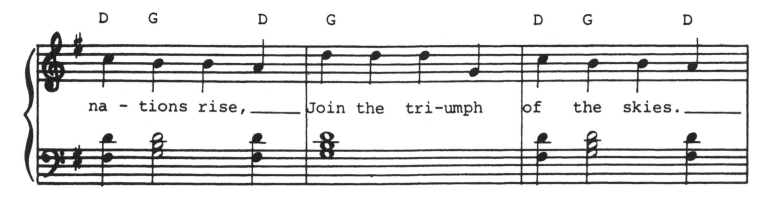

na - tions rise,_____ Join the tri-umph of the skies._____

With an-gel-ic hosts pro-claim, "Christ is born in Beth-le-hem."

Hark! the her-ald an-gels sing, "Glo- ry to the new-born King!

He Leadeth Me

Our Father In Heaven

He's Got The Whole World In His Hands

Steady moderate beat

He's got the whole world in His hands, He's got the whole wide world in His hands, He's got the whole world in His hands, He's got the whole world in His hands.

*(1) He's got the earth and sky, in His hands,

* 2nd time: Land and sea, wind and rain, spring and fall.
3rd time: Young and old, rich and poor, Yes He's got ev'ryone
in His hands.

His Yoke Is Easy

Holy, Holy, Holy!

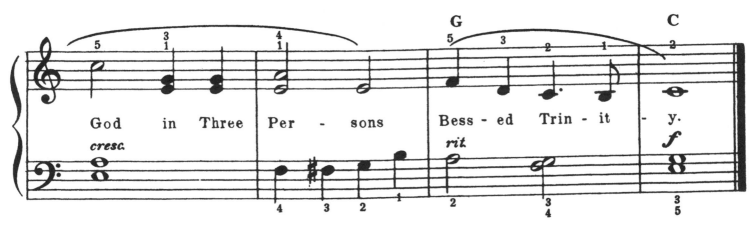

Hymn To Joy

Con moto (spirited)

2nd time:

Sing! Sing a Hymn To Joy,

In ev'ry heart may joy abound.

Make the hymn a song of joy,

From pole to pole the world around.

Life can be beautiful when the value of love
        is understood,

Sing! Sing a Hymn To Joy —

To Peace, to Love, to Brotherhood!

I Am Praying For You

Andante

I have a Sav - iour, He's plead - ing in glo - ry, A

dear lov-ing Sav-iour, tho' earth-friends be few; And

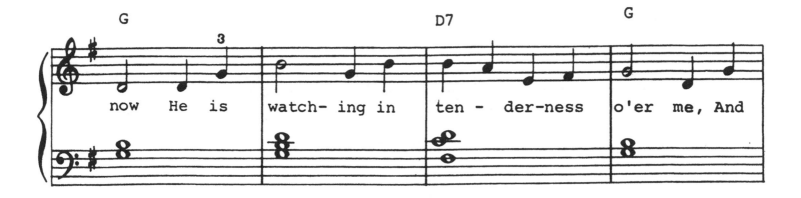

I Love To Tell The Story

Moderately

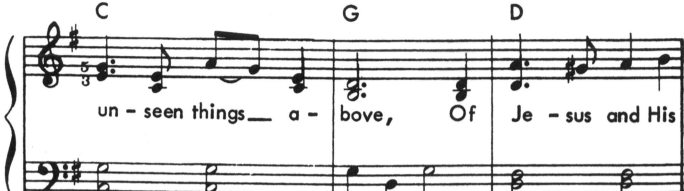

How Gentle God's Commands

Moderately

I Need Thee Every Hour

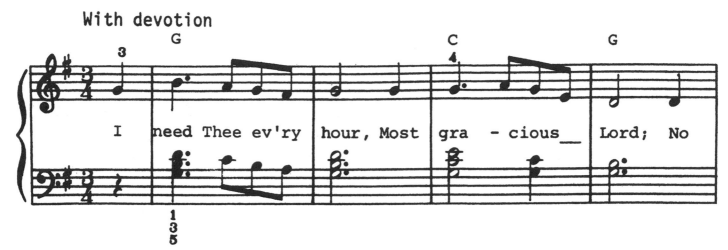

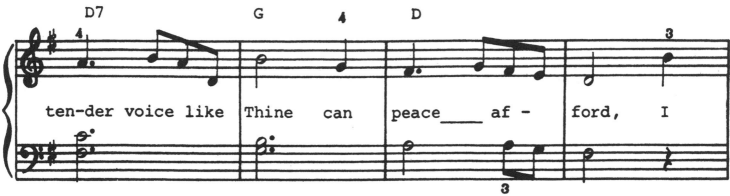

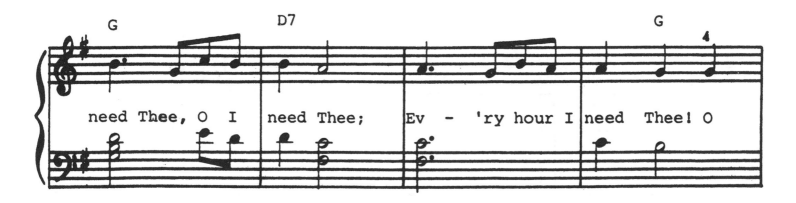

In The Cross Of Christ
I Glory

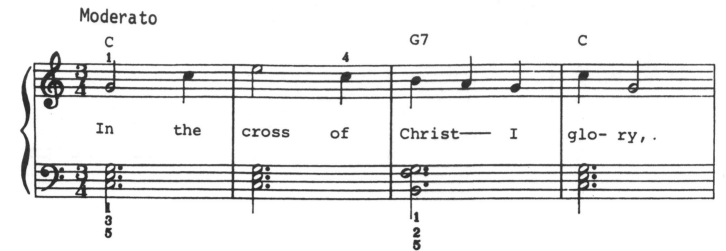

In the cross of Christ— I glo-ry,.

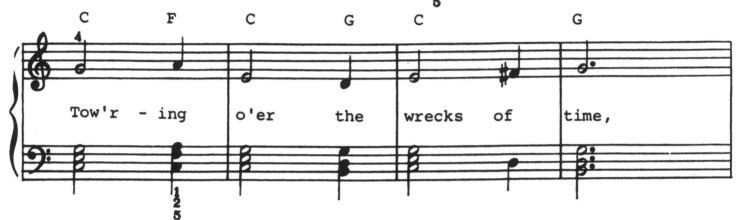

Tow'r - ing o'er the wrecks of time,

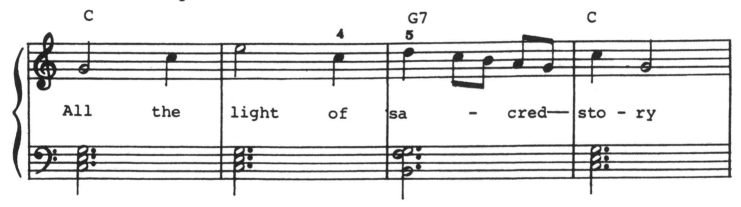

All the light of sa - cred— sto - ry

Gath - ers round its head sub- lime.

In The Sweet Bye And Bye

I Think When I Read That Sweet Story

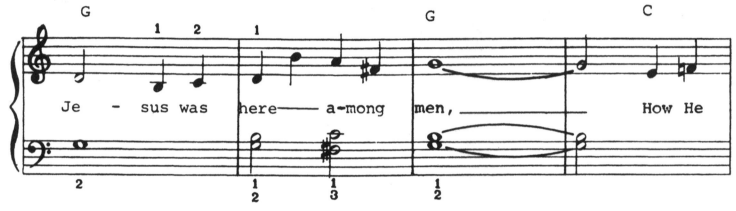

Kum Ba Ya

Moderato

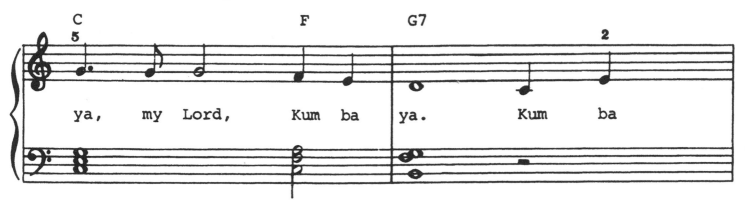

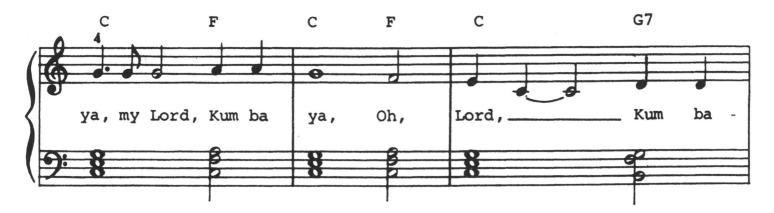

Jesus, Lover Of My Soul

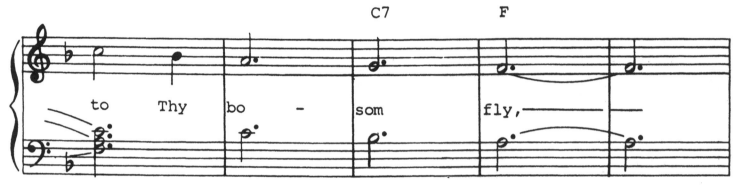

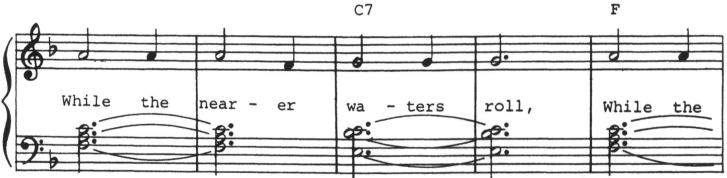

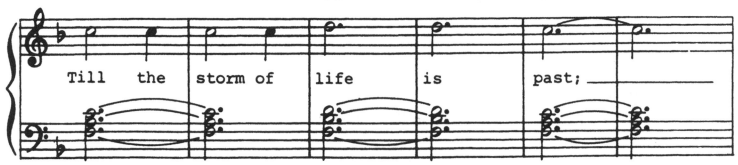

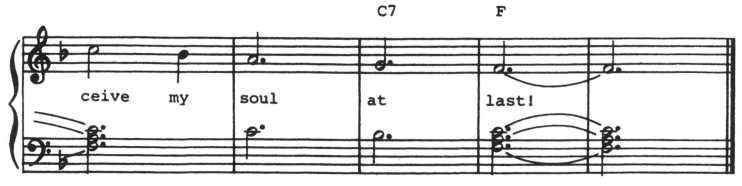

63

Jesus Loves Even Me

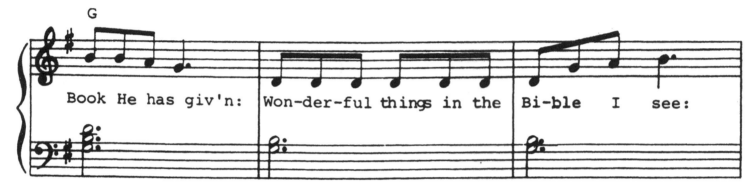

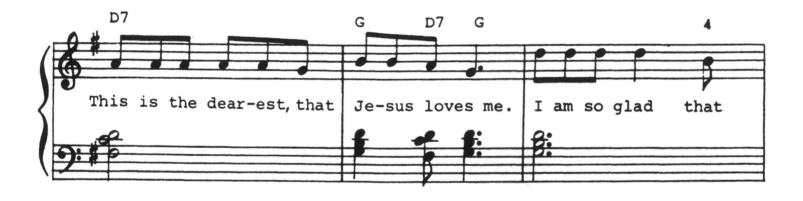

I am so glad that Je-sus loves me, Je-sus loves e-ven me.

Jesus Calls Us

Joyfully

Je - sus calls us o'er the tum - ult Of our

life's wild rest-less sea, Day by day His sweet voice

sound - eth, Say-ing: "Chris-tian fol-low me."

Jesus Saves

Joyfully

We have heard the joy - ful sound: Je - sus

saves! Je - sus saves! Spread the ti - dings all a-

round: Je - sus saves! Je - sus saves! Bear the

news to ev-ery land, Climb the steeps and cross the waves; On-ward!

'tis our Lord's com- mand; Je - sus saves! Je - sus saves!

May The Grace Of Christ

Moderato

May the grace of Christ our Sav - iour And the

Fa -ther's bound-less love, With the Ho - ly Spir-it's

fa - vor, Rest up- on us from a - bove. A - men.

Jesus Savior, Pilot Me

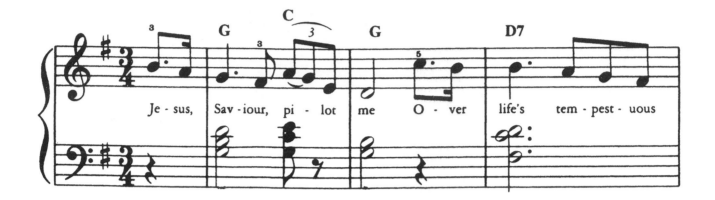

Je - sus, Sav - iour, pi - lot me O - ver life's tem - pest - uous

sea; Un - known waves be - fore me roll, Hid - ing

rock and treach - 'rous shoal; Chart and com - pass came — from

Thee: Je - sus, Sav - iour, pi - lot - me.

Jesus Shall Reign

With praise

Je - sus shall reign wher- e'er the— sun

Does his suc- ces - sive jour - neys run;

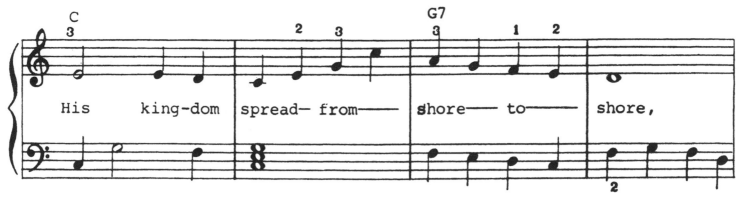

His king-dom spread— from— shore— to— shore,

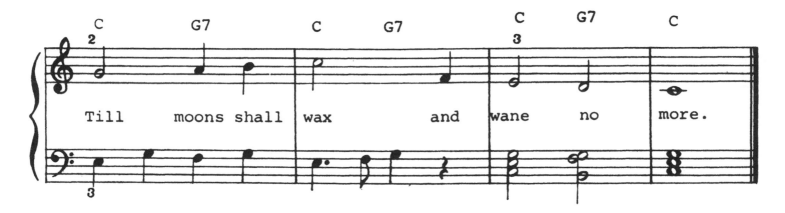

Till moons shall wax and wane no more.

Joy To The World

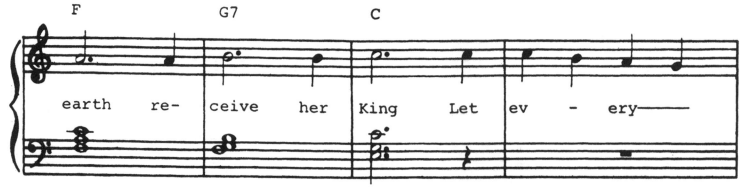

Holy, Holy, Holy (Sanctus)

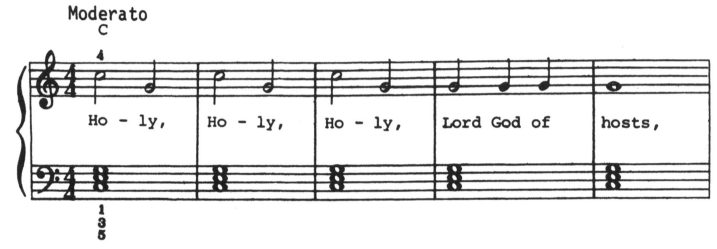

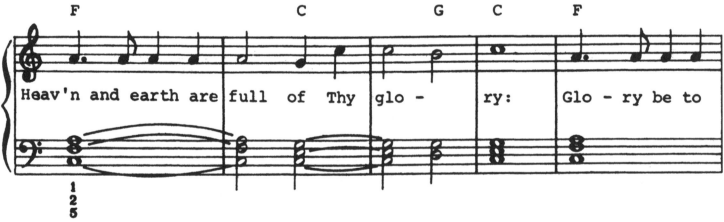

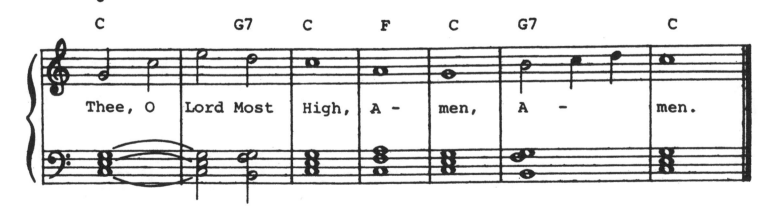

Just As I Am

Quietly

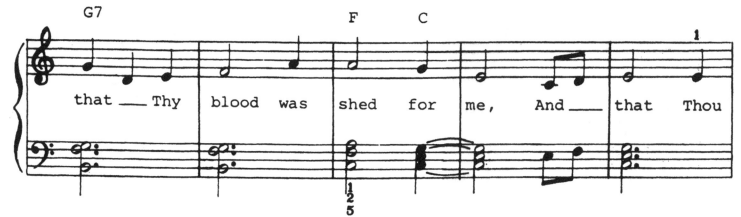

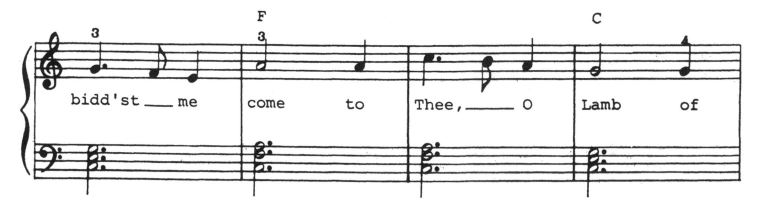

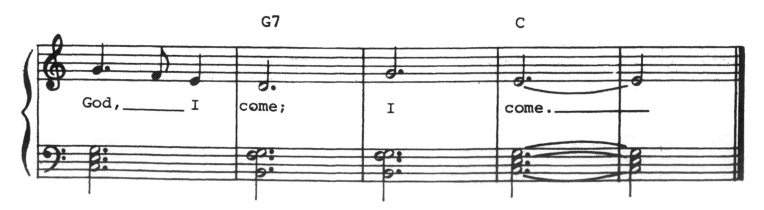

Lead, Kindly Light

Jesus, Keep Me Near The Cross

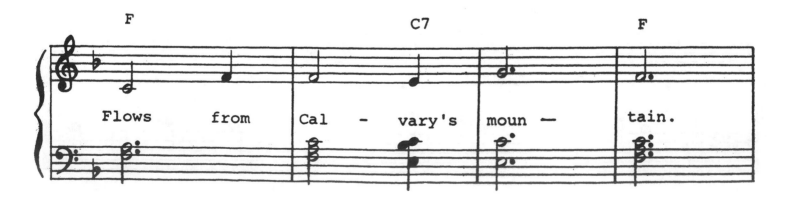

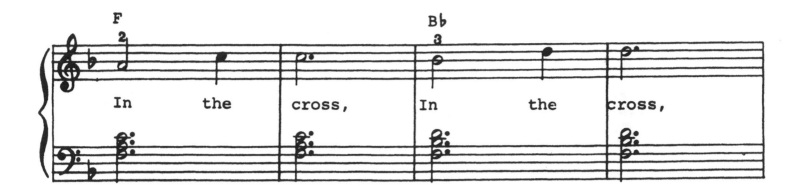

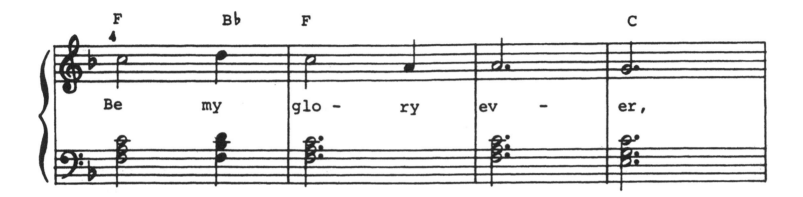

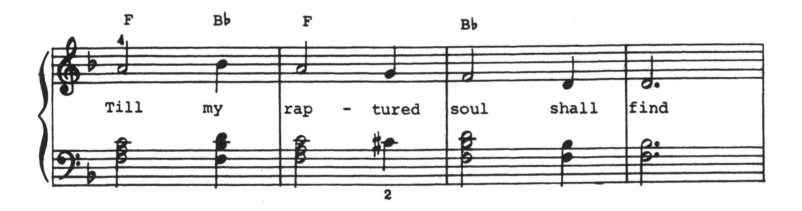

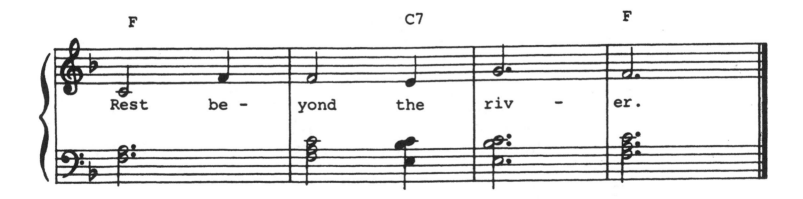

The Little Brown Church
In The Vale

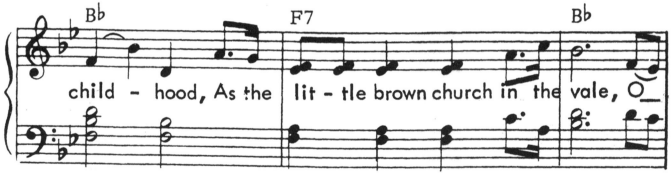

child - hood, As the lit-tle brown church in the vale.

Our God, Our Help

Moderately

mp Our God, our help in ag - es past, Our

Hope for years to come! Our Shel - ter from the

storm - y blast, And our E - ter - nal Home!

Lord, I Want To Be
A Christian

More Love to Thee

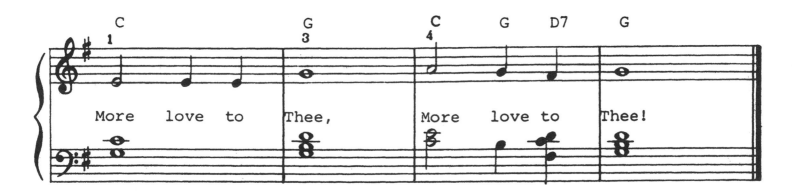

Mary And Martha

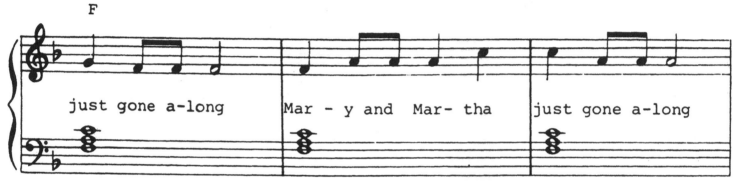

C7   F

Free grace, un- | dy- ing love, | Ring them gold- en | bells.

Hear Our Prayer, O Lord

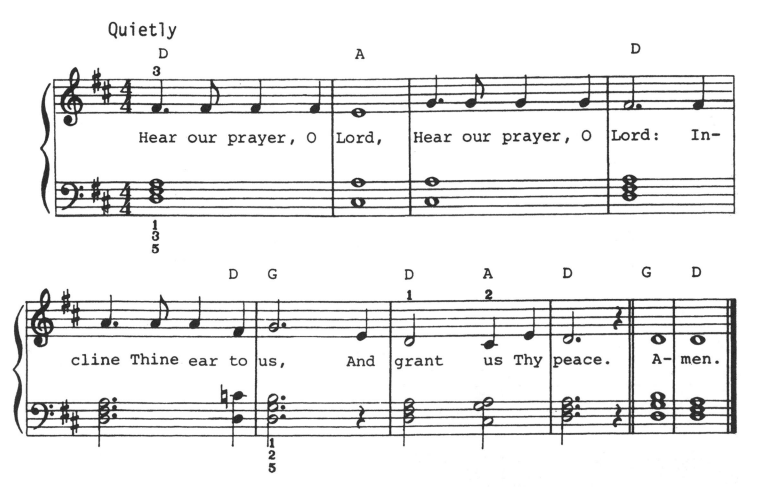

Quietly

Hear our prayer, O | Lord, | Hear our prayer, O | Lord: In-

cline Thine ear to us, | And grant us Thy | peace. | A- men.

My Faith Looks Up To Thee

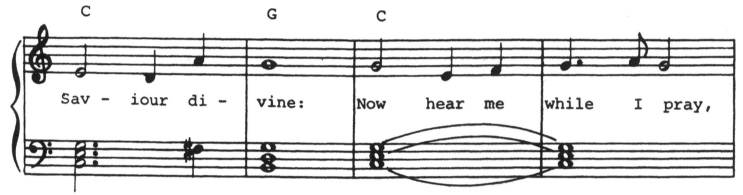

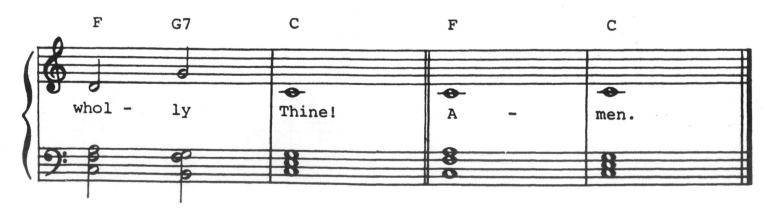

My Jesus, I Love Thee

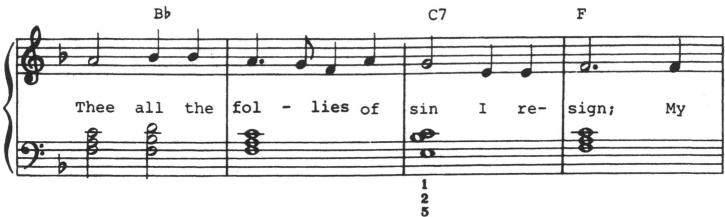

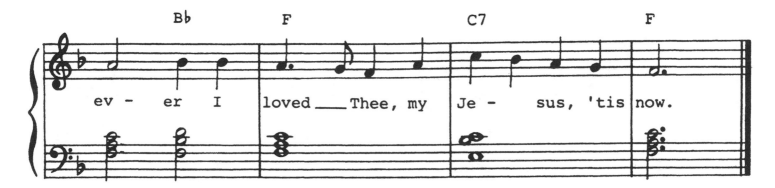

Nearer My God To Thee

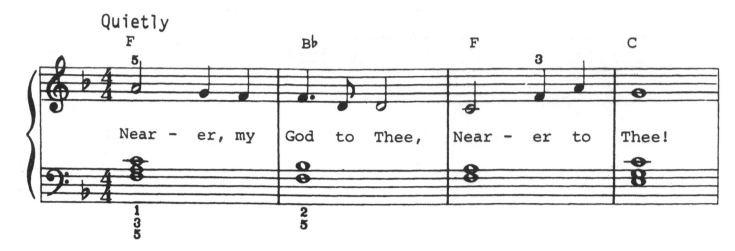

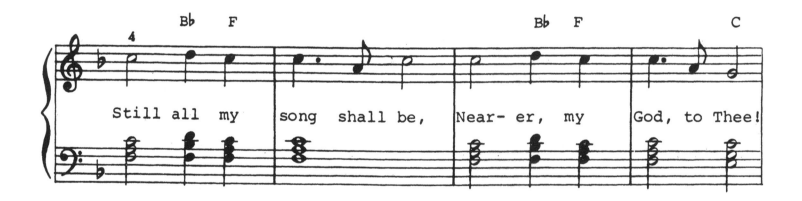

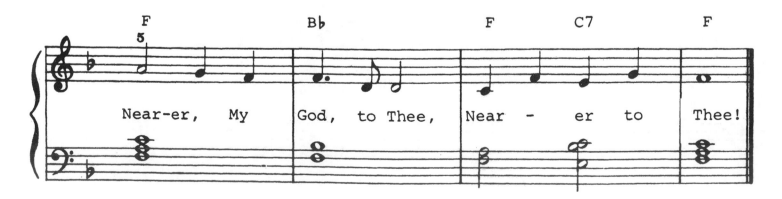

Now Sing We, Now Rejoice

Now Thank We All Our God

With thanksgiving

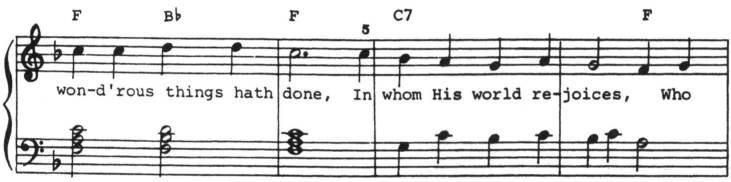

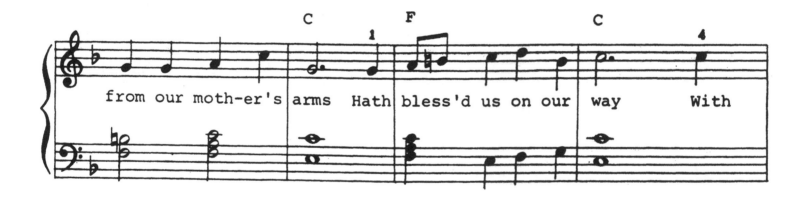

O Day Of Rest And Gladness

Moderato

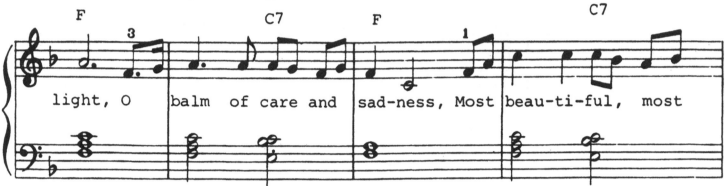

O Beaulah Land

Lively

I've reached the land of corn and wine, and
all its rich-es free-ly mine, Here shines un-dimmed one

bliss-ful day For all my night has passed a-way: O

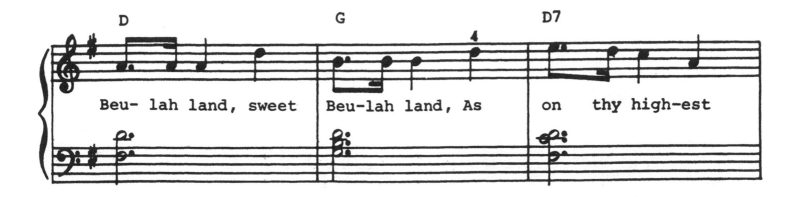

O Come, All Ye Faithful

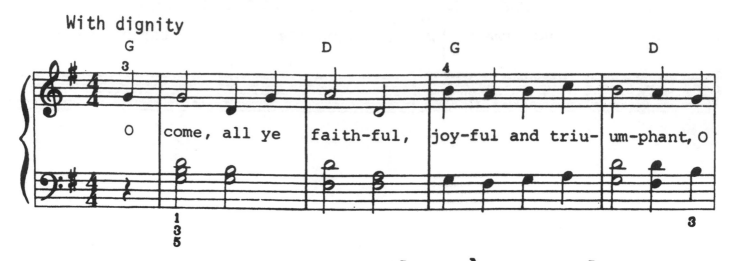

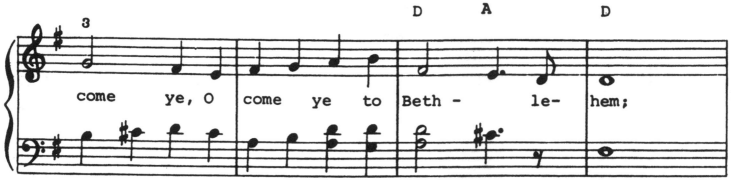

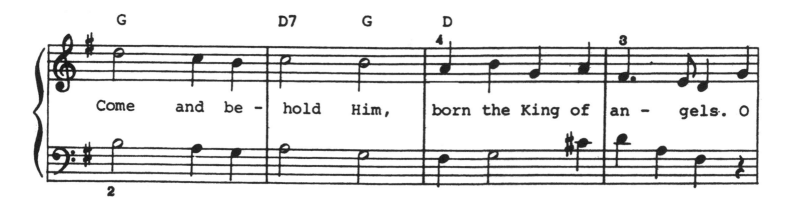

come, let us a- dore Him | Christ, the Lord.

As Each Happy Christmas

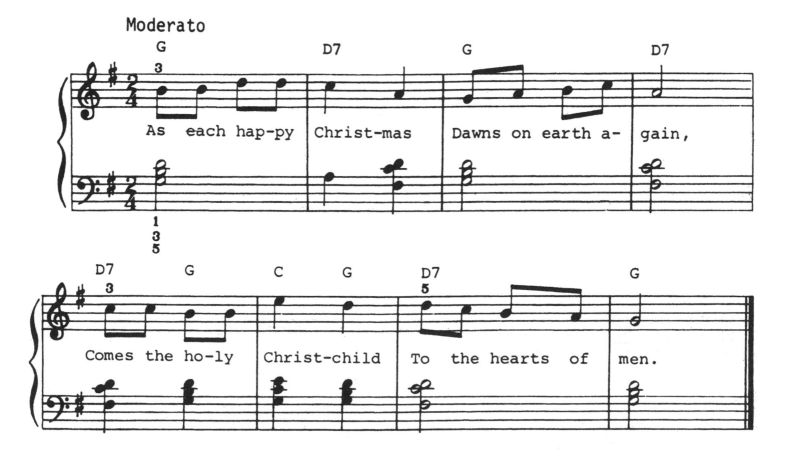

Moderato

As each hap-py | Christ-mas | Dawns on earth a- | gain,

Comes the ho-ly | Christ-child | To the hearts of | men.

O Happy Day

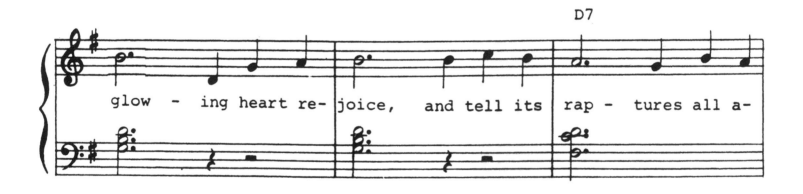

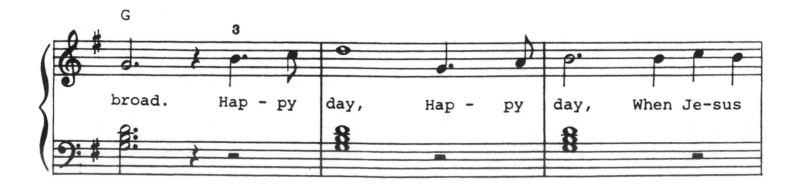

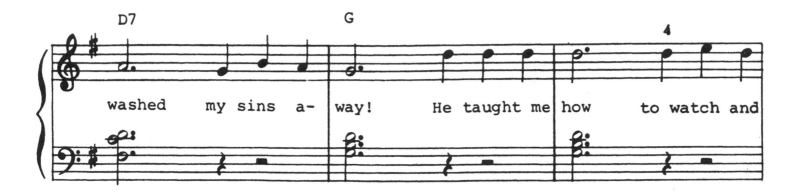

D7   G   4

washed my sins a-way! He taught me how to watch and

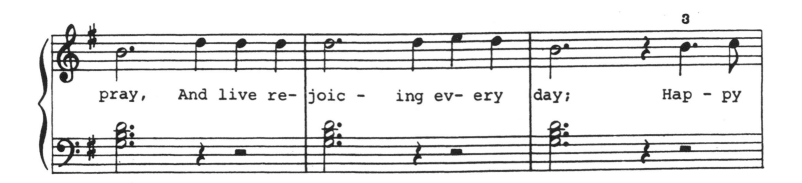

3

pray, And live re-joic - ing ev- ery day; Hap - py

D7   G

day, Hap -py day, When Je- sus washed my sins a- way!

Once In Royal David's City

eyes at last___ shall___ see Him, Through His own re - deem - ing___

love; For that Child so dear___ and___ gen - tle. Is our

Lord in heav'n ___ a - bove, And He leads His chil - dren

on To the place where He ___ is ___ gone.

O Perfect Love

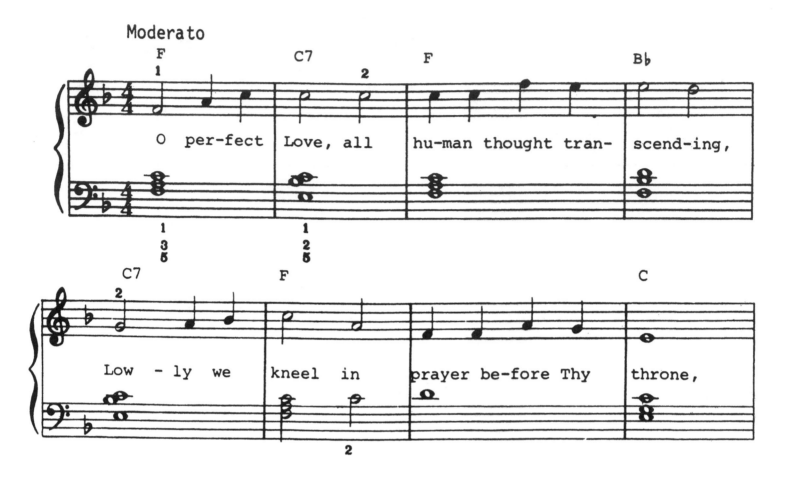

Praise Him Evermore

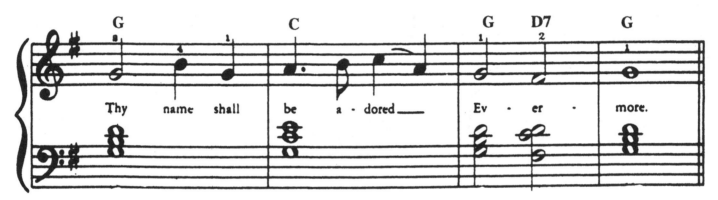

Praise Him, Praise Him

With praise

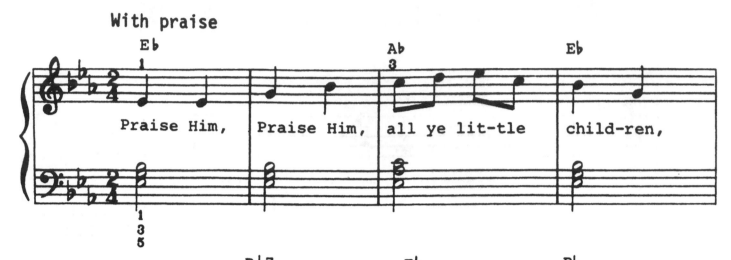

Praise Him, Praise Him, all ye lit-tle child-ren,

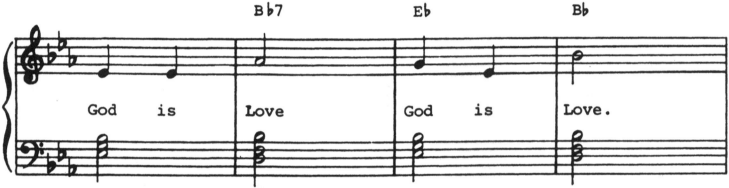

God is Love God is Love.

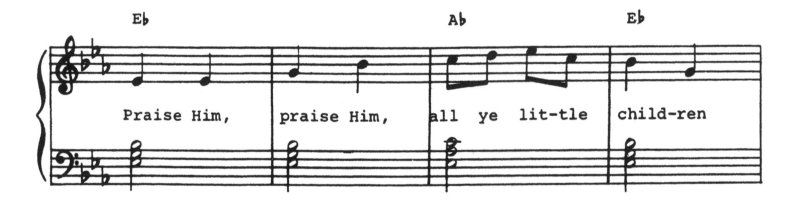

Praise Him, praise Him, all ye lit-tle child-ren

God is love, God is love.

Rock Of Ages

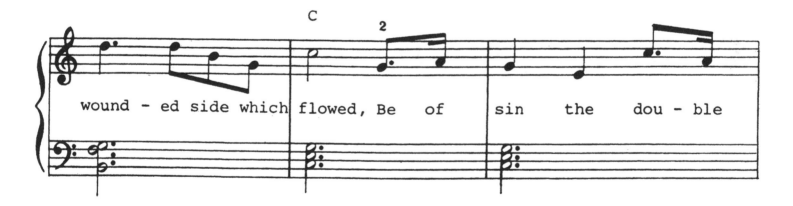

Send The Light

Joyously

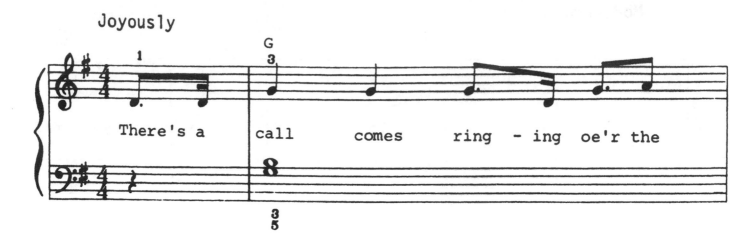

There's a call comes ring - ing oe'r the

rest -less wave, "Send the light! Send the

light!" There are souls to res-cue, there are

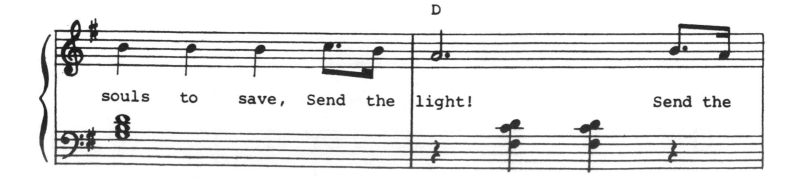

souls to save, Send the light! Send the

Silent Night

Quietly

Si - lent night! Ho - ly night!

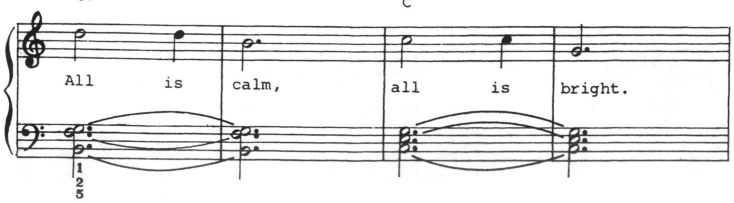

G7

C

All is calm, all is bright.

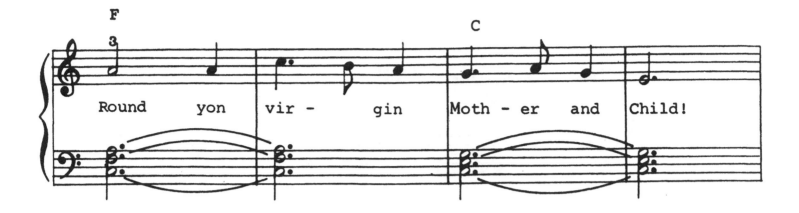

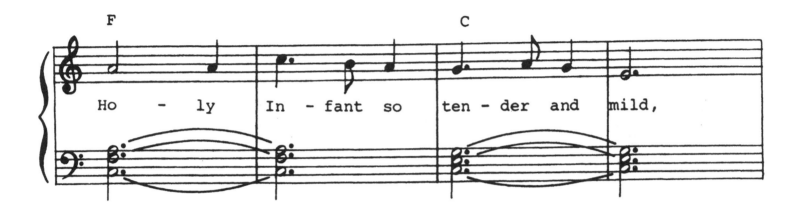

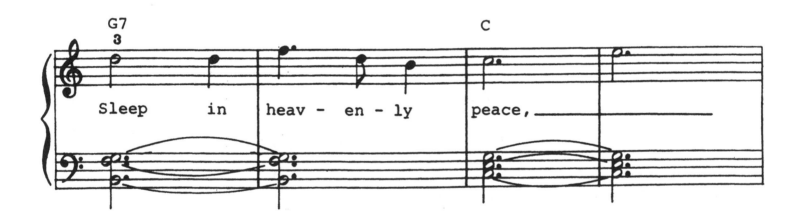

Stand Up For Jesus

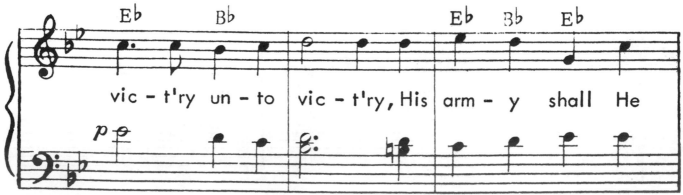

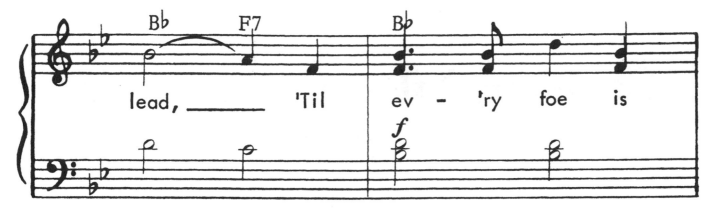

lead, _____ 'Til ev - 'ry foe is

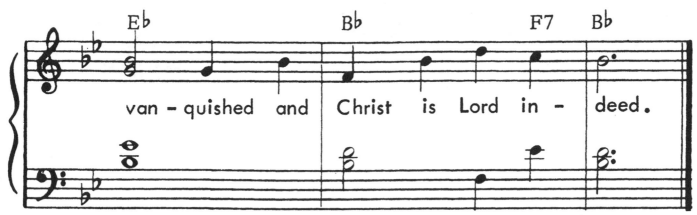

van - quished and Christ is Lord in - deed.

Peace, Perfect Peace

Calmly

Peace, per-fect peace, in this dark world of sin? The

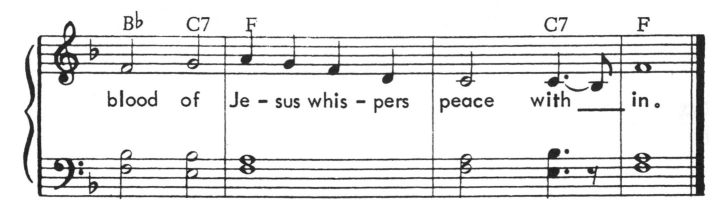

blood of Je - sus whis - pers peace with ___ in.

Saviour, Like A Shepherd Lead Us

Sun Of My Soul

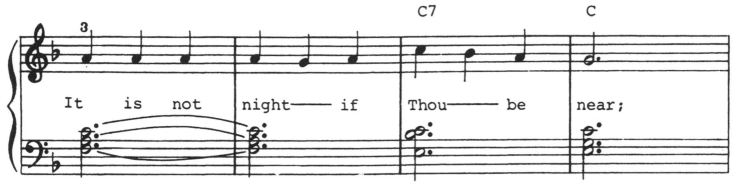

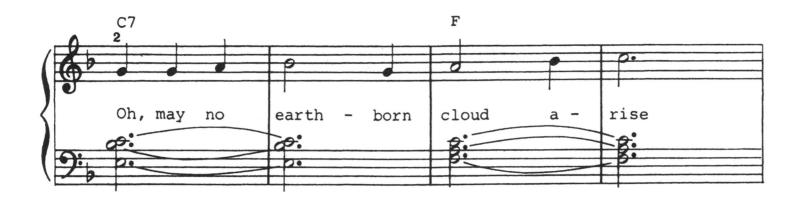

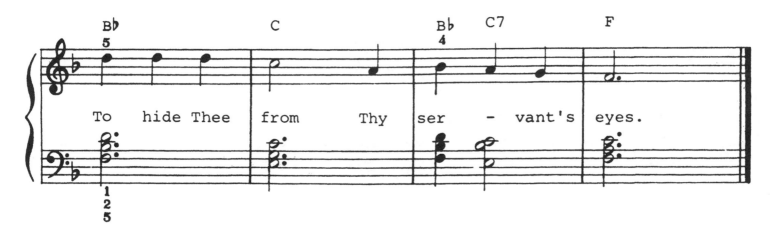

Sweet Hour Of Prayer

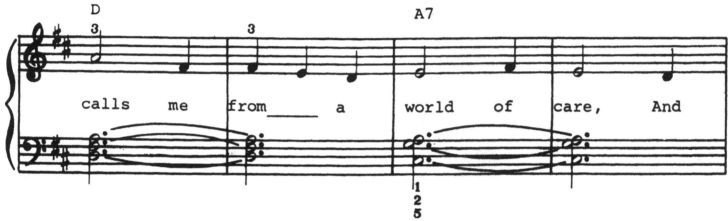

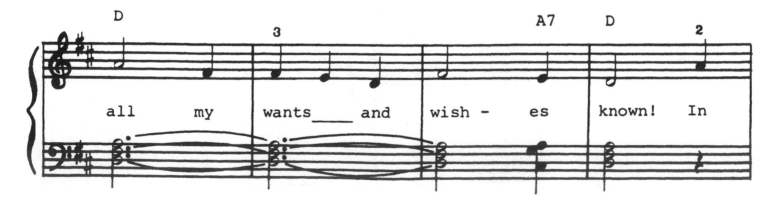

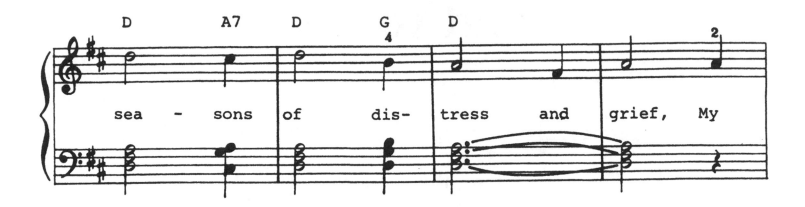

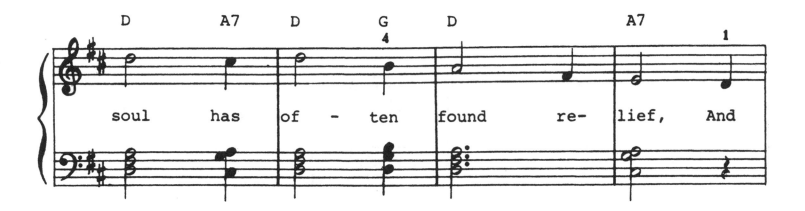

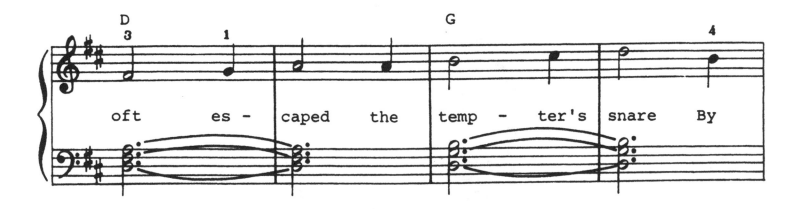

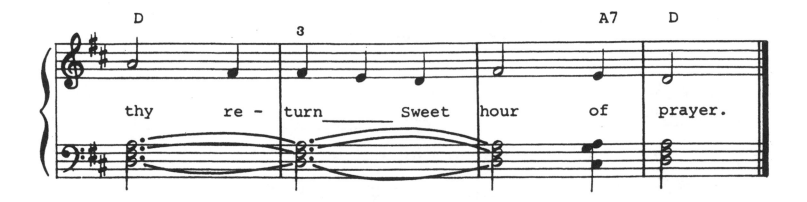

Ten Thousand Harps
And Voices

The Lord Is My Shepherd

cresc. et ritard

Up From The Grave
He Arose

Were You There

there when they laid Him in the tomb?

O Love That Will Not Let Me Go

Moderate

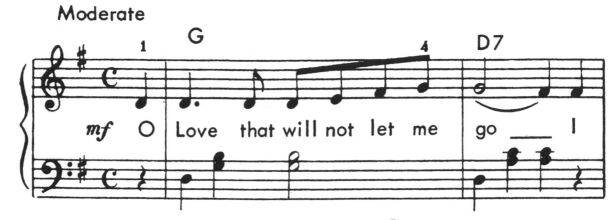

mf O Love that will not let me go, I

rest my wea - ry soul in Thee,— I give Thee back the life I

owe,— That in Thine o - cean depths its

flow, May rich - er, full - er be. A - men.

Walk Beside Me, Precious Lord

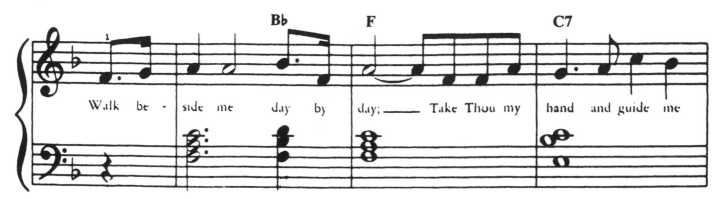

What A Friend We Have In Jesus

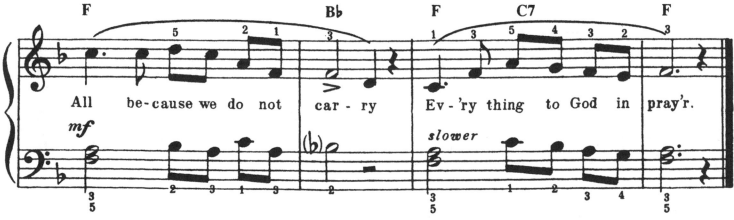

What a friend we have in Je-sus, All our sins and grief to bear!

What a priv-i-lege to car-ry Ev-'ry thing to God in pray'r!

O what peace we oft-en for-feit, O what need-less pain we bear,

All be-cause we do not car-ry Ev-'ry thing to God in pray'r.

When I Survey The Wond'rous Cross

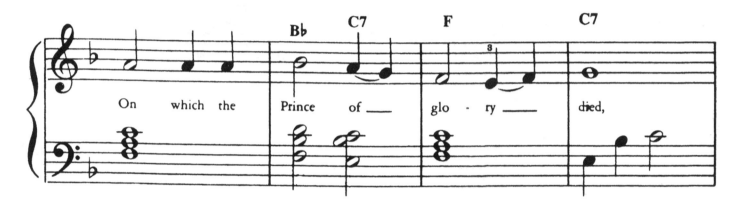

When I sur-vey the ___ won-d'rous ___ cross

On which the Prince of ___ glo-ry ___ died,

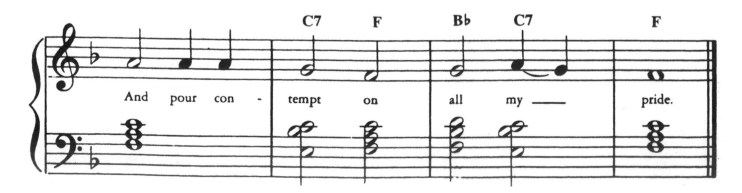

My rich-est gain I ___ count but ___ loss,

And pour con-tempt on all my ___ pride.

While Shepherds Watched Their Flock

Whispering Hope

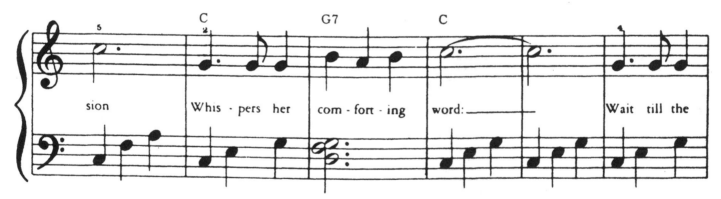

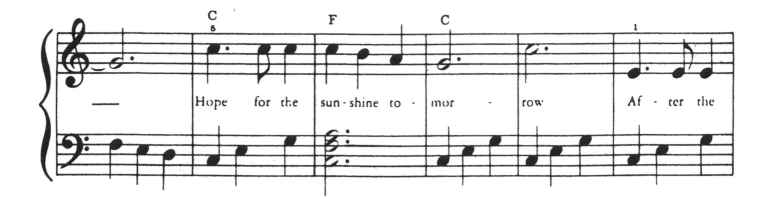

Wonderful Words Of Life

Joyously

Sing them o-ver a- gain to me, Won-der-ful words of

Life: _____ Let me more of their beau - ty see,

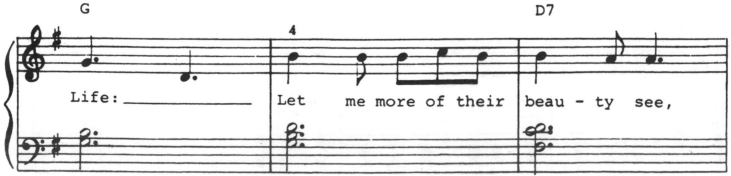

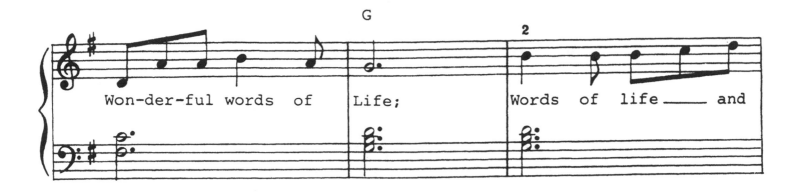

123

You With Your Wounded Hearts